# V
# T
# The Windmills



## Jim Adams

This book is not an autobiography. Although the stories did happen they did not, necessarily, happen to me. I have merely put the events and people from different times and places into one 'life time'.

Braiswick

To my long-suffering wife,
children and friends

Other books Jim Adams

Samantha - a love story
The Last Great Hockey Player
Even For an Eggshell
Begley Bottom
The FY System
The Funny side of the Fourth Estate
PAUNII
Return to Paunii
Bimmy the Barber Vol. 1 to 20

**Braiswick**
Felixstowe, Suffolk

ISBN 978-1-898030-16-4



British Library Cataloguing in Publication Data available.

Cover design by Eileen Aldous

Printed by Lightning Source
*Braiswick is an imprint of Catherine Aldous Design Ltd*

## Acknowledgements

Especially Robin, my accountant who will be eagerly waiting to see if anyone buys a copy in £'s Sterling.

And John, so that if I become rich I will buy another car from him and he can then stop patching up the old Merc.

The girls at the Abbey must be told that if I become rich they will no longer have to lend me their lunch money to pay my overdraft.

And finally to my publisher, who hopes if this sells millions I will stop sending all these sodding manuscripts!

## About the Author

Very little is known about the author simply because very few people actually care.

A Colonial of little repute, he lives, temporarily, in England, in Suffolk, to be geographically accurate, with his long suffering wife and the occasional visit from his children.

He is an old man who works at various things, including writing for the odd newspaper, and putting together various mountains of written rubbish in the forlorn hope that some deluded publisher may take pity on him and put some of it into print.

You could also say about him is that he loves old dogs, children, and watermelon wine, though not necessarily in that order.

Although he has about him the demented air of the reformed alcoholic, he drinks very little, smokes the odd cigar, and eats most things, and has a fondness for bacon sandwiches.

# Chapters

You may have noticed there is no list of Chapters, as found in most other books.

This book is not like other books. If you need to know which page a chapter is on don't be so lazy, go look for it.

I don't know which page the chapters are on, so why should I look through the book and list them when it's just as easy for you to look yourself.

That's the trouble with the world these days.

People are too bloody lazy.

They want everything done for them.

So there!

# CHAPTER ONE

I am not annoyed at every thing in life. I am only annoyed at the things that annoy me – and that is almost every thing!

I mean just look at the childhood I spent. On the farm we had to get up early, work like shit and then go to school – I mean I was just a kid, not fair is it. MY kids won't get up in the morning even when they have to, and I can't really blame them; but I do. Lazy little toads.

I used to spend all my spare time skating, this wasn't very easy because the ice wasn't always there and when it was other people were using it. Or it was melting. Or it was the summer and there wasn't any ice. Life is a bitch. I mean take Tom Crumback.

Tom Crumback and his mother, father, sister and all the hired help lived on the next farm to us – the house was about half a mile from ours and it was big and covered in shit most of the time. It wasn't entirely their fault, the Crumbacks I mean, because they let their cows wander all over the place whereas we didn't. But then if they DIDN'T let their cows wander all over the place the stupid things wouldn't shit everywhere, would they!

Any way, Tom Crumback, now there was a miserable son of a bitch if ever there was one. He was my age or maybe just a bit older than me, and he was my best friend at the time. We played ice hockey together for the village team and he was bigger than me, fatter, and meaner, so every time I played against him in practice he used to charge down the ice at me – even if I didn't have the puck, and he would smash into me at about fifty miles an hour (well, OK, 25 miles an hour) and whack me up against the boards, and I can tell you it hurt like shit!

Cows are such stupid creatures, I mean they don't look where they shit, everywhere, even when you are milking them they lift up their tails and the bloody stuff, all wet and shiny and stinking, splats all over everything – milk should come in bottles, like it does in the city then we wouldn't get so covered in shit all the time. No wonder farm kids stand out at school; you can smell them. Mind you, nearly all the kids at our school were farm kids so it didn't really matter. I thought ALL kids stank of shit, when a new kid came to school and didn't stink of shit I used to think there was something wrong with them – like little Dolly Booth, she didn't stink of shit, even after I had grabbed her and kissed her she didn't stink of shit, and I only did that because Billy Haigh bet me I wouldn't. Come to think of it he still owes me a quarter for that. Tight bastard.

The Crumbacks were nice people really, Tom's sister, Betty-Lou had a kind of crush on me. Well she didn't really but I wished she did, I fancied her like crazy, she had these big tits, well they weren't really big, but she never wore one of those things that keeps them under control so they looked big, and she used to let me squeeze them sometimes. Any way, Betty-Lou was quite pretty really and she was fun to play with. She used to come skating with us and we used to have Weiner roasts and corn roasts on the ice at night, all the kids in the village used to come to them, they were fantastic, but not as much fun as the parties we used to have on the corn fields, when it was warm; or when we used to go skinny dippin' at the lake, that was fun, and my god I can tell you there was some squeezing and kissing and fumbling things that went of there, I can tell you. She used to stink of shit, Betty-Lou I mean, but I didn't really find that out until after I left the farm and went back many years later. God did she stink of cow shit. But she was really pretty when she was older, and her tits were really big, and she still didn't wear one of those things for keeping them in check – or whatever.

Anyway, what was I on about, oh yes, leaving the farm. Well I didn't really want to stay on the farm. It was fun, OK, I enjoyed it, and I had lots of friends, but it was all that work, and all that shit.

Anyway, I got me job playing hockey in the big city, now that WAS fun; and the money was better than on the farm, sometimes. I mean there were times when the money wasn't so good. There was a time when I played for a small team up in the mining towns. I played for this team - the Wanderers, and the winter was so bad hardly any one could get to the games so we didn't make much gate money and they couldn't afford to pay us much, it was really cold that winter, we used to set fire to things just to keep warm. Anyway we, the team and me, found that we could get a job in the lumber camps- well not exactly because they thought we were a bunch of idiots because we came from down south, but they did tell us that there was a stand of trees that needed taking down, they offered us about fifteen hundred bucks if we did the job - roots as well.

OK so we cut the trees down, and we cut them into lengths and we burned off the branches, but since the ground was frozen down to about three feet we couldn't get the stumps up.

Anyway, this Provincial Police man told us we would need dynamite, he said that there was some dynamite in the shack about four miles into the woods, and he said he knew nothing about it and we guessed, rightly as it happened, that he didn't want to know!

Anyhow we found this case of dynamite and we hammered a crow bar into the ground around the stumps and we put a two-inch fuse into the dynamite and shoved a stick down the hole. Well a two inch fuse wasn't nearly long enough and since we had cut down all the trees there was no where to hide.

The second stump we used a foot of fuse. That was better.

Andy Duval still limps, fifty years later. Then this Forest Ranger came along and when he looked at the dynamite we had used – there was only a stick or two left – he stood there. Looking at us and scratching his head. "You lot are fuckin lucky you aren't all dead, don't any of you know anything about dynamite?"

"Well yes," said Barney, our captain, "used it on the farm."

The Ranger looked at him, like he was some kind of eejit, "On the farm you used agricultural dynamite, this is different, this stuff is sweating, is could go at any time, the nitro is oozing out of the stick!"

That's something ELSE they didn't teach us in school, boy that really pisses me off!

# A CHAPTER ON FARMING

We had a big farm, 'bout five hundred acres, well there were bigger farms, but at my age, to me, I mean, it was a big farm. We had a very big barn, made out of corrugated tin with iron girders and things, we stored the hay and straw in that barn and when we were kids we used to play in it when it was raining or snowing. Had swings and all kinds of things - made castles out of the bales of straw. It was brilliant, until I got caught with Jane, but that is just too embarrassing and I will skip that episode.

We had some old trucks, they were pretty well beaten up but they still ran, after my brother fixed them, and we used to bomb around the fields with them. Well it saved ploughing!

Halloween was a great time of the year, we used to do some fantastic 'trick or treats' in those days, one year, '53 I think it was, a kid in another village got shot. Well it was his own fault really, dressed up in a bear skin and wandered around the farm yard, he spooked the cows and the farmer, an old bloke by the name of Clarkson, shot him with a 12 gauge, killed him. Didn't do the bearskin any good either.

Most fantastic thing we ever did was to old Arnie Westbrook. We took his hay wagon apart and put it back together again on his barn roof. Took us nearly all night and we fell off a couple of times, but I guess they are still talking about that these days!

Then there was Stuart, my god, what a character he was. Tall, gangly, long hair, big nose. Well Stuart weren't thick or anything, but he wasn't very bright either. He could eat a ton though, anything you stuck in front of him he ate.

Never quite sure where he came from. We were like that, with all my brothers and sisters and cousins and things we always had a house full – big house too, eight bedrooms and a small flat next to the dairy. Anyway, I never did discover who Stuart was, or where he came from, or who invited him. One day he just appeared and he stayed for about three months!

We had this well up in the fields above the house, there was a big brick shed over the well and a huge tank over the top of it, and we used to have to pump water from the well into the tank so that it could run down to the house. Stuart used to do most of the pumping, while he was there. I think that was why he came. Maybe God sent him, or something, any way, although we were supposed to take it in turns we all used to call out "Stuart, your turn to pump!" and off he would go. Trouble it he got carried away and didn't know when to stop. I went up to find him one night after he had been gone over an hour, and there he was, tank overflowing, water pouting down all over the silly bastard, and he was singing, can you imagine that, SINGING hymns, or something! Crazy bastard. He was OK though, I quite liked him. Couldn't skate worth a damn though.

There are a lot of things you come across when you are growing up, some of them are nice things, mostly they are nice things, sometimes though, and this does happen quite often, there are things that aren't so nice – like school.

Mostly I liked school, the kids were OK, mostly they were kids I had grown up with so I knew them pretty well; the teachers were local folk, village and town folk, so I knew them pretty well, it was just that school seemed to take up an awful lot of time, we always seemed to be at school, well, not always, I mean we were at home and at play, and on the ice, and other things, but it was just that at the times I really didn't want to be in school I had to be. Take Jo-Anne Pfeiffer, now there was a girl, trouble is Jo-Anne came from Guelph ; her Dad brought her to school and took her home again. It just wasn't fair. She couldn't go to school in Guelph because of some trouble so she had to come to our school, and I was crazy about her, yet the only time I saw her was at school and in the play ground, and you can't get much courting done in a playground with all the teachers and kids watching. I wasn't old enough to drive then so I couldn't visit her and she wasn't allowed to come to our hockey games because of all the swearing and stuff. Being ten years old just ain't much fun. Trouble is by the time I had grown up enough to see Jo-Anne she had grown fat and had freckles.

We had a lot of pigs and chickens on the farm, and geese, and cows and horses and other things. We had to feed them and clean up after them all the time. You would never believe how much shit a calf can leave around, pigs too, messy bloody things. And we had to clean up after them all the time. Crap!

I walked through a cemetery the other day; it brought me down to earth with a thump. Then I got thinking, Time, Space, Infinity, Forever, what does it all mean? If we are able to travel back in time, would we be able to meet all those people again? I don't really think we can ever travel forward in Time, because if we did, I mean if we were to go ahead in Time to Christmas 2222 it wouldn't be the future any more, would it. The second we got there it would be the present, and a second later, the past! So we would never actually be in the future, would we? It would always be the past! Or the present.

Something my Granny always told me, 'you can't have your cake and eat it.' - can you?

Anyway, in this cemetery with all those dead people, and all those things written on the tombstones. I got to thinking, what would I want on my tomb stone - suppose you could put what you want on your stone while you are still alive, what should I put?

And then I got to thinking about Australia . Did you know that once, millions of years ago, Australia was at the North Pole? Then the whole shooting match slipped down where it is now. That is weird! Polar bears in Sydney. Definitely weird.

# A CHAPTER ON JONAS

I had a mate once, Jonas; I forget his last name so I will call him Jones, well Jonas Jones (not his real name, you understand!) was as nutty as most of my friends were/are. He used to think that one day he would be rich and famous, that he would write a book and sell the story to Hollywood and become a millionaire. Well he did, and he is. Now that is really weird. I mean at school he was a plonker, he was full of shit, I mean he always pretended he knew more than any of us, well, actually, he did, but he didn't have to keep telling everyone.

Anyway, Jonas, he was Welsh, no, that's not quite right, his father was Welsh, from Welsh Wales. He used to keep on about it all the time, telling us what a beautiful voice Welsh people had. He used to sing in the choir on Sundays, in the church, and he did have a lovely voice, Jonas's dad, not Jonas, Jonas couldn't sing at all really, well, just a little bit.

But what he said is quite true, I have been to Wales and they can sing lovely voices. Haven't a clue what they sing about because they sing in Welsh.

It's a lovely country Wales, full of hills and sheep and old stone houses, and trees, I love trees. But all the towns and villages have funny names that are very difficult to pronounce, except Bangor - they have Bangor in America, south of the border, it's in Maine, but they all speak English there, well, American anyhow.

The Welsh people all want to leave Wales , they all want to go and live in Australia . Now there IS a funny country. Everything in Australia will try to kill you, all the fishes - sharks, jelly fish, snakes, spiders and other insects, plants, animals; everything is poisonous, deadly, ugh! Even the women (they call them Sheila down there), they will get you if you let them! Beautiful country though. They have some funny names there, places like Wogga Wogga, and Sydney.

Trouble with Australia you can only live in the bits around the outside, rest of it is dry and full of kangaroos and things - and people driving around in 4 x 4's looking for water and gold and Sheilas. But the bits around the outside are very nice, except for the snakes and things. They have mountains and rivers and lots of nice sandy beaches full of crocodiles (which will also want to eat you, the Aussies don't feed them, they let them have the odd tourist).

I had this Australian friend a long time ago, he was a tall, tubby feller, full of beer and beef, he dressed like a tramp although he was worth a dollar or two. Never worried about anything other than the price of oil and the fact that the fridge had only twenty-four tinnies left in it. Never worried about anything that is until his hair started falling out.

"Struth Mate, me bleedin hair's fallin out." He would scream, "Look at it, all over the fuckin place, jeeze, what a bummer!"

And, sure enough, his hair was falling out. One or two to start with, then, after a particular long and tough drinking session, ten or twelve at a time, used to fall from his head to his shoulders then onto the floor - with scarcely a sound. Just like that. Worrying.

His name was Bruce, no, what wasn't his name really, but because he was from Oz we called him Bruce. Actually we called him lots of things, especially when he stuck his size 12's on the table, or farted at dinner, or belched at breakfast, then we called him some pretty horrible names, I can tell you. We should have chucked him out but he paid for everything and since we were all broke most of the time, it was nice to have someone pay for everything even if they did fart all over the house. The house, that is, where five young, single hockey players stayed while we were looking for girls suitably mentally unbalanced enough to go with us beyond the 'hop into bed' stage. We were all hopeful that one day we would get a proper job - as out parents kept telling us to do - and find a 'nice girl' and settle down. Well. We weren't particularly hoping to do that, but our parents were all we ever wanted was a couple beers, a quick leg over and "just give that shirt an iron before you leave darling!"

One of the main things essential for the playing of ice hockey, in fact, THE main thing you need is ice. Back in the days when we worked and lived on the farm the only near ice was about eight miles drive away, and that ice was dependant on the outside temperature. The nearest indoor ice rink was even further, and until we were able to drive either legally or without getting caught without a licence, we had to rely on others to get us to the rink and back again. However, as it used to be in Ontario , in those days, one was assured of plenty of ice from the end of October onwards.

It wasn't always that easy though, having ice was fine, first to had to make bloody sure that it would be strong enough to hold the weight of a dozen hefty farm lads, to do that involved finding someone enough of a mug to venture first onto the lake.

It was about five years before I cottoned on as to why the others took so much longer than me to put their skates on. I wasn't quite so bright in those days!

Eventually we rigged up a stone gate post with a long rope, the rope was attached to the post and the other end thrown across the ice, we then pulled the post over to the other side, if the ice held and didn't creak, and we knew it was safe. The post weighed about a ton so it was a safe bet.

The years after the Second World War were strange years, old fashioned, yet bang up to date. It was a mixture of the pre-war times, the times when money counted - especially if you didn't have any! And there was plenty of work.

There was plenty of sadness too, grieving, husband and son-less widows and mothers. Broken hearted young girls whose boyfriends and fiancées didn't come back. Half empty dining room tables. Un-driven cars rotting in garages; empty hooks on the back door; un-filled places at the factory benches.

It was shit really, why did people feel the need to kill people?

I used to walk around cemeteries, looking at the gravestones, seeing if I could spot the ones who hadn't died naturally. People didn't put things like that on grave stones, just things like "Born 1876, Died 1905. Loving Husband and Father. Rest in Peace.

Rest in Peace, there's a good one, how the fuck can you 'rest in peace' when you died so young, so unfinished, so much to do?

I used to look at these poor sods' gravestones and wonder what God was thinking about, letting them die like that. And children, why do children have to die?

I used to call out to God and ask Him, "why did you let it happen; what the fuck did they ever do to you?" Then I would get scared and tell Him I was sorry, just in case.

We were scared of God in those days, had it drummed into us at school and at church, "Fear God", obey, behave, do as you are told. Confess your sins!' That used to crease me; I was thirteen for Christ's sake, what fecking sins can a thirteen-year-old commit? I just used to wish I could have some sins to confess to! I mean I used to kiss, cuddle and feel up girls skirts when they would let me, and I used to have wicked thoughts about some of them, even Miss Dooley, our music teacher, she had these gorgeous legs and she always wore short skirts and if you were quick when she sat down…!

I think she did it on purpose, they would call her a real poser these days, then we just called her a very desirable bit of nooky, though none of us ever tried it on with her, we were too scared of adults in those days, they could cane you for almost any excuse, and they did. Sadistic bastards, some of those teachers.

I could understand that if God had made too many people, and they didn't all fit on to the world, He may have needed to pick a few off, but if that is the case why not just make it so that not so many are born? I think I would sooner not be born than to be bumped off!

It is not as if the world is all that crowded. All the people in the world at any one time wouldn't fill Loch Ness! And all that land in Australia- shit, there are miles of it; even Canada has a lot of space no one lives in, and South America, and Africa , I mean the world is full of empty spaces.

It's like everything else in life, just as you learn to do it well - you don't have to do it any more. That is Stupid!

The only trouble with the space in Canada - as my old Dad used to say, "It's full of holes!"

Which is quite true, fly over Canada on a clear day and it IS full of holes - lakes! Canada has lakes it hasn't even used yet, big, small, shallow, deep, warm ( in the summer) and cold in the winter - frozen - mostly! Which probably accounts for the fact that most Canadian kids skate!

The populations of the countries in the world are very unbalanced; they need shaking up and redistributing. Instead of all the major cities having millions of people, and all the countryside having hardly any, they should take some of the city slickers and make them live in the country!

I just cannot understand why anyone would want to live in London, New York, Tokyo, Berlin, Moscow, Mexico City or any other smog-bound metropolis, shoulder to shoulder with smelly, heaving people, in smelly, overcrowded slums, Yuk!

There are few nice cities - Montreal, Edmonton, Melbourne, Vienna, Helsinki, Rio de Janeiro, Caracas, and Buenos Aires, but even they have their faults, poverty, crime, corruption etc.!

# NONSENSE CHAPTER

Lots of things in life don't make a lot of sense. Take distance. You get born and brought up in one country, and as soon as you get old enough you bugger off to another one. In order for you to do that some poor sod had to invent boats and planes. They cost money and use up fossil fuels to run them. If every one stayed where they were we could save a fortune.

Even walking -shoe leather; riding - horses and things, bicycles, automobiles, buses, trains - just think of the money we could save if we all stayed home?

My first car, one I owned myself, was a Model A Ford. Circa 1932. It had running boards, a lift up windscreen, and a crank handle to start it, a hand throttle, advance/retard spark lever, a manifold heater, and precious little else.

Lizzie, as I named her, had no antifreeze, in the winter I had to fill the radiator up with a kettle full of hot water before I could crank her up; she started first time - every time!

If it was snowing I had to either hand operate the wipers or open up the window. Because the heater didn't work unless you were travelling fast

(30 mph), you had to dress up very, very warm. In the summer, however, she was a darling, lovely and cool!

Lizzie had nearly bald tyres but she ran fine, over snow or sand, and I had more fun with her than any other car I ever owned. In the winter I used to make $5 a time push starting newer cars.

Lizzie wasn't very fast or powerful. With a full load on you had to either reverse up a hill or get out and push. I did that often, leave the old girl in first and pull the hand throttle up a bit then jump out and push. You had to be pretty quick jumping back in when you reached the top of the hill!

Henry should have kept making Model A's, they were the only good car Ford ever made, but they were good.

I nearly went into business with a friend of mine. He had been trying to buy his mother a cut-wood coffee table. The only ones he found were $449 more than the $1 he could afford. On his way past a sawmill he watched them cutting up timber and asked them if he could buy some four-inch rounds cut off a big log of green oak. He bought 10 at a dollar each and we loaded them into and on top of Lizzie and took them back to his farm.

The idea was to sand them and polish them then add some varnish, put legs on, and sell them at a vast sum of money in the town.

After the bloody things had sat in the sun and rain for a week they all split into cheese size wedges - very expensive logs!

# ANOTHER CHAPTER

Tell you something that gets right up my nose – this religion thing. I was brought up to fear God. Bang, that was it! Fear God, worry about eternal damnation, worry about the Heavy Hand of God that will strike you down if you tread the wrong path! Step out of line and God will get you, as sure as He made little green apples!

And who told me all this? The Father. Not MY father, Father Tobias to be exact. He told me.

So for the first few years of my life I feared the Wrath of God.

I didn't LOVE God, how could I, I was scared bloody stiff of Him.

As I grew older, I grew a little wiser, too.

Father Tobias lived in a big house. The church was a fecking big church. It was covered in lovely ornaments, expensive goblets, candlesticks and other bits and pieces (at least the insurance company was told they were expensive after they got nicked!). Then when I started visiting countries where there were simple people, peasants, and poor people who had very, very little of anything, I found that they were giving ten percent of all they had - and that was almost ten percent of feck all! - To the church. Churches that were, just like Father Tobias's church, filled with gold and jewellery and candlesticks.

The final straw came when I visited a big Abbey and saw the entire finery that the Bishops, and Cardinals, and even the Pope had.

I mean, why do they need all that wealth, all that show of wealth?

Back 2,000 years, did Jesus have all that money, all that wealth - gold candlesticks and things? Did he shit? Poor old Jesus had feck all. And most of that He gave to other people. So why does the church today have to have all that wealth, all those magnificent buildings, buildings like St. Paul's, the Vatican, Ely Cathedral, Lincoln Cathedral, Wells Cathedral, and all the other really beautiful Cathedrals, not just the ones in Britain but all over the world there are rich, wealthy churches and cathedrals.

And millions of starving people.

And how is it that all those guys in their fine robes and trappings proclaim that THEY know the will of God? I doubt it, I doubt it very much. If I was God and I wanted to contact the people I had put on the earth I would choose someone I could trust and depend on, not some fancy dressed up pious blokes. How can they absolve a person from sin, by what right do they do that? And if they say it is the 'Will of God', I say, prove it !

# YET ANOTHER CHAPTER!

Memory! Now there's a nice kettle of fish.

One of the most confounded things in the world is memory.

Memories keep coming back at the wrong time, they go just when you need them, and they crop up just when you try to forget them.

You always seem to lose them, and it takes a very small thing to bring them back - sometimes they hurt when they come back.

I have often thought that God should have had us born old and grow younger, and memories are just the reason I feel that way. Instead of having to look back we could look forward. I don't really know what we would be looking forward to, without memories we would have nothing to look back on!

I can understand why we need memories, after all, when you get older and lose your memory you go down to the mall to get some eggs and things and then forget why you went. So we need a memory just to remember that much! What I can't figure is why we have to remember all the things we learned in school hundreds of years ago, and yet can't remember a couple of eggs and a pint of milk! That is weird.

And dreams, what is that all about? You work hard, play harder, have meal and a drink, and then go to bed minding your own business and whoops, before you know it you are knee deep in dreams. More weird stuff.

Nightmares – another weird thing! I love smelly cheese. In fact I could eat smelly cheese till the cows come home. The smellier the better. Trouble is it makes me dream like shit.

And do I have some dreams! If only my dreams could come true, just a couple of them! Wow. All those young girls I went to school with...Wow. That barmaid at the Rose and Crown, the fallen Madonna with the big boobies...Wow.

No, wouldn't want it really, let them stay as dreams.

Spoke to a chap the other day, his wife was very ill – and blind, and his daughter aged 48 had just died. He didn't want any dreams either...or memories.

Life is a Bitch, as they say. I will have to speak to the Big Guy when I see Him, one or two questions I really have to ask Him.

## CHAPTER 13

New Zealand, now there's a funny country. Rains a lot and the folk that live there are very nice. Very big, very rough and hard, very good at sports and have a funny habit of rubbing noses. Apart from that…

Oh yes, the country is almost empty, I mean there are hardly any people living there and the ones that are born there escape and live every where else. You meet Kiwis all over the world, they travel none stop until they are worn out then they go back to New Zealand to rest and to watch rugby and cricket, to drink quite a bit and eventually drop dead.

The Kiwi, their national bird/emblem is a shy little bird that can't or won't fly. There aren't many of them left, and that is not because they have all left, but because you won't find them anywhere else in the world.

Every one who makes films/movies wants to make them in New Zealand, probably because it is the loveliest country in the world with really spectacular scenery – you know, mountains, lakes, trees, rocks, clouds, rain, warm, cold, volcanoes, earthquakes (about twenty every day!), hardly any dangerous animals (except on the rugby field), but they have to take their own extras with them as there are very few people living in the country!

Most films made in the next twenty years will be made in New Zealand probably so if you want to be in the movies go and live over there. You do, however, have to like sheep - both as friends and as food and clothing - they have millions of them. And if you want to ever really made a Kiwi (the people, not the birds) mad ask them 'what part of Australia do they come from!' But as soon as you ask the question run like shit in the other direction

# MICHELLE - AN AUNT

This was to have been a chapter about my Aunt Michelle, only she wasn't such a bad old girl and I didn't want to labour on about her and the few faults she may, or may not have had! Michelle was not her real name, that was Josephine, she called herself Michelle when she opened up the whore house in Los Angeles , shortly before her husband

Uncle Cecil caught her in bed with the hired help.

No, Cecil was a randy old sod so I am very surprised that she still had any strength for a bit on the side, still, she was an attractive wench.

Michelle, or Josephine, as we all called her, decided that if she was going to get laid every couple of hours she may as well get paid for it, so she moved from British Columbia down to Los Angeles and opened up the cat house. It wasn't long before twenty girls from the farms joined her and she soon had such a roaring business Uncle Cecil forgave her and moved down to LA to keep her company, bonk most of the girls for free, and bank the money.

Well to cut a long story short, after they had a couple of million in the bank, Cecil turned Michelle - or Josephine- in to the law and went off to Hawaii with the youngest of the hookers. Last I heard he was still there!

Michelle - or Josephine - did two years in the pokey and came out only to open up another cat house in San Francisco this time. She then married again, telling the beak that her husband was dead - killed by a beer truck running over him -only this time she married a man with tons of money who shagged her every night and paid her so much that marrying her was the cheapest way out. He was Chinese and owned a Chinese restaurant. Michelle - or Josephine - loved Chinese food and spent most of the evening eating with the customers, she then spent all night in bed with Wong Fu paying for it!

Last I heard she shagged the Chinaman to death and now owns the restaurant where she now lives with the head waiter - another Chinaman.

# CHAPTER NINE

I hate hospitals, doctors and ugly nurses - in that order.

Hospitals are full to the brim with sick people. You have only two ways to leave a hospital, walking or feet first.

It is possible to go into a hospital with a headache and never come out again, or come out with many more complaints than in you went!

Doctor's surgeries are just as bad. ONLY sick people go to see a doctor, and boy, are they sick. More germs, viruses and microbes live in doctor's surgeries than anywhere else on earth; the places are full of them, everywhere. Ugh!

It is probably the main reason why doctor's receptionists are so hard-nosed and unfriendly. The have to be to keep the people far enough away so that they don't catch anything from anyone.

Dentists are different. Have you noticed that the most beautiful girls in any town all work in dentist's surgeries? Do you know why that is? It is to stop you behaving like a big girls blouse when the dentist comes at you with a fecking big needle and says something really stupid like; 'this won't hurt'.

It does, it hurts like hell; it hurts like some medieval torturer pinching your balls with red-hot pincers. It hurts like some one piercing your tongue in order to put a stud in it - as all the girls do these days. It hurts like shit!

Hurt is a funny thing; it can come in many different guises. Hurt and pain can hit you at any time and in many different ways.

Pain can be physical - a blow to the head, a smack on the rear end, a doctor's needle.

Or it can come at you when someone you like snubs you; belittles you; turns your world upside down.

I was only sixteen when I got hurt like that. I thought she liked me, I really thought she liked me loads. I had skated with her, taken her out to barbecues, been to parties with her. I dreamed about her every night and spent hours on the phone with her every night for month (our local calls were all free!) and then just when I joined the team I had prayed I could one day play for, she dumped me - for the captain of all people. God I hated that bastard, I hated him so much that at the first opportunity, in practice, I put him in hospital. But she still wouldn't go out with me again. Bitch. I did get some sort of revenge, she married the captain and he turned out to be a real bastard, beat her up a few times – though I was sorry about that, I didn't want that to happen, but she left him and several years later she married a sailor, moved to Australia, he found some gold and now he is dead the bitch inherited all his wealth, forty million bucks. Shit!

Still, it could have been worse, she could have married me and I could have inherited some wealth – would be nice, not a lot, just a few million would do.

# A CHAPTER ON DREAMS

## (Or what happens when you eat too much cheese)

I dream a lot. Nothing strange about that, you may think, but to me it is important. I need my dreams. I love my dreams.

I even used to have nightmares. Although I could never understand why they are called 'nightmares', I don't remember ever dreaming about horses, mares or stallions.

I have dreamt of all kinds of things. When I was young I used to have lots of dreams about girls. Wow, yes, Wow. Some of them. Mostly I dream about cars that don't seem to run properly, or muddy car parks and fields. I always have lots of friends in my dreams. And often family.

I had a dog that used to dream, she would lay on the floor by the fire and strange little sounds would come from her, she would whimper, growl, make funny coughing sounds, and her little ears would flick and toss – her whole body shaking with either delight or dismay. She never told me what she was dreaming about; but then she never really told me anything. Strange dog.

I visit strange houses and shops, places that are very familiar yet completely strange, place I know, and know well, yet I can't put them into anywhere I know now – as if I have lived another life and yet have all the memories of both lives. Weird!

# THE 'BIG BANG' CHAPTER

## (And I don't mean Jenny Rogers!)

I read a very informative book the other day, a book that makes me really, really wonder. Bill Bryson - the best storyteller around, stated that before everything that is anything came along there was nowt (as they say in Yorkshire ) Now I don't just mean empty space, or even a vacuum, there was NOUT! Nothing, not even an empty space. There was no TIME, no planets, no universe, no stars, no air, no chemicals, NOTHING. Not even the minutest atom that today are so small millions would fit on the full stop at the end of this line.

Think about it. Before the BIG BANG nothing existed. You can't even say that nothing existed for millions or even billions of years before the BB, because if Time didn't exist then you have no way of measuring anything. I mean if you had been around in those days you would have needed one hell of a lot of patience! But then...

I often try to think of nothing. My mother used to say that was all I ever thought about, but then she was like that...or I was.

Anyway, this 'empty space' thing, trying to imagine nothing is very difficult. Even 'empty space' is something, but to imagine something less than that...well!

And this BIG BANG, if there is NOTHING where did the things(s) that caused the Big Bang come from in the first place, they must have been lurking around behind the bookcase or somewhere, I mean you can't just have nothing and something at the same time. Unless the neighbours sent it over, you know, 'here, you've got nothing, so have a cup of big bang to go with it!'

I've worried about this for years, just can't get my head around it!

And distance. They tell us that the Universe is expanding at the speed of millions of miles per second, everything is rushing away from everything else – quickly, yet when you look at the stars and things they don't seem to have moved very far since I was a kid – and that's an awful long time ago, I can tell you!

Now if you look at a car doing a very slow (by space ship standards) 60mph it is really moving, you can see it, right? But the stars, travelling at millions of miles and hour don't seem to move at all! Am I going bonkers?

No,- this space malarkey is something else, I can tell you!

Another thing, all these black holes. They are so dense (knew a kid at school like that) that a star that implodes shrinks to the size of a pea and weighs billions of tons! Come on! A plate full of peas like that balanced on your knife! Then eventually they become so dense that not even light can escape from them. If this is true, how the hell can you see the f...ing things!

And IF they are that powerful I just hope we don't have any in our back yard.

# YET ANOTHER CHAPTER

I have a bone to pick with the BBC regarding the TV licence.

It is now free to old people OVER 75. Great! At 75 you are too old to watch TV. Everything on TV is a repeat, so old that we old people have seen them all several times. When you reach 75 all you want to see is young things - preferably wearing skimpy clothes and no knickers. All you get on the TV (BBC anyway) is repeats of old films with all the 'young things' wearing bloomers and cast iron bras. Or black and white melodramas, or black and white war films; or science fiction with all the space ships dangling on bits of very visible string; or cowboys who get in a fight and never lose their hats and manage to get off five hundred rounds without reloading their six shot pistols; or fifty long legged girls dancing on the wing of an aeroplane while it is flying over South America!

And we need to see them all again?

When some of the old films were made Charlie Chaplin was ten and Frank James was still alive!

Come to think of it not such a good idea, they shot back at you.

I am going to be (in my next life) a film-maker. I am going to move to Africa and film all the insects, elephants, tigers, crocodiles, monkeys and those funny little critters that stand on their hind legs and look for lions that Attenborough missed in his last film series. I now know more about the Serengeti than I do about my home town - thanks to him. And when I've filmed all those animals - that always come on at dinner time - just when I am about to tuck into a steak and kidney pie you see a fecking big lion ripping the guts out of a poor bloody antelope - and then I'm going to shoot the fecking lot of them, lion and all.

We are living in an age of the SIGN. Everywhere you look there are signs, I bet that even in the Serengeti there are sign that tell the animals what to do, like to cheetahs chasing zebras' KEEP LEFT. STOP AT CROSSROADS! Or to tell others, BEWARE LOW SWINGING MONKEYS! Or to the gazelles and buffalo, KEEP OFF THE GRASS! Any day now I expect to see a sign in the park that says; IT IS FORBIDDEN TO THROW STONES AT THIS SIGN!

Oh, by the way, I am not keen on a sentence that is why I use mostly paragraphs, very few sentences. I believe that it makes it easier to read when you don't have to keep looking to see where the next bit starts.

But then I could be wrong!

Too many signs, too- many instructions, too many orders. Life is slowly being planned for us, next thing you know all birth certificates will have an expiry date!

Why can we not just be allowed to get on with it, to find our own way through life, to wander among the hills and valleys of fear and trepidation, to experience the thrill and the fun of the chase - and the catch? Why can we not be allowed to learn through trial and error of the path we tread through life?

The odd muddy foot - the time we tread in the dog shit - does it matter? Is it not our foot?

The things we learn in life - sometimes we learn by hardship and the mistakes we make - are the things we treasure most. What we learn, and pay for, we come to respect the most. Take away the learning and you replace these things with mistrust and a careless disregard, "that which is lightly earned is little valued".

We have grown up; we don't need nannies any more. To the State I say, 'leave us alone', feck off, let us make our mistakes and pay the price - or earn the reward thus gained.

# A SAD CHAPTER

Some things make me sad; it must be the Irish in me, the sentimental Irish that always makes me weepy through the sad bits in films or TV.

One of the things that make me sad is the thought of anyone alone, alone and with problems, and no one to help them. Must be terrible that, all alone and no one to turn to, that makes me really sad, and a little angry. WHY should any one be alone and have no one to turn to?

It happened to me once, many years ago, and it was quite horrible. Only once and it was my own fault, but it did give me an idea about how miserable it can be - being alone.

I know a lot of people like that - lonely people, old people who lost a partner; young people who got kicked out by their parents, or through parents dying, that is really terrible, really, really, terrible.

And then you see pictures of all these kids in Africa - they have no parents, no friends, no help, no hope...and we think we have problems?

Must be the Irish in me.

I want to help them. I can do nothing. Why are we all so helpless? Is this what it is all about? No wonder people go out at night and kick gravestones over.

What are THEY trying to tell us?

Should we care? Should we care!

I am just reading a book about a man who hitched around Ireland with a refrigerator. Now why the feck would any one do that? For a bet!

I did some weird things for a bet once, back when I was young and stupid. People are like that - not young and stupid, but doing bets - when they are young, and old. I still do crazy things for a bet. IF the wager is big enough! But that is something else.

Every day I meet people who are lonely, I even meet and hear about kids who have no one, kids tossed out onto the street by uncaring parents, now that's a bummer, just who the hell, I mean what kind of parents could toss their kids out? It makes me fecking mad to think that there are people out there who could behave like that, poor little sods, just what the hell could a kid have done to be chucked out of their home. It beggars belief.

That's not the only sad thing. I watched a programme about the Tsunami that killed all those people at Christmas 2004. It is heart-breaking, soul destroying. The feeling of helplessness as those who lost family and friends, standing on the shore, or on top of buildings - safe, while those around you die in the muddy, wreckage strewn water...

But then life is like that. I mean every time you turn around there is some big, mean ugly bastard waiting to nail you...if you let them.

# CHAPTER 300

We went for a long walk the other day. The sun was shining and the sea gulls were squawking and the other people walking near us were making more noise than the gulls.

The vendors on the beach were selling fresh caught, deep-frozen fish (and how can that be?), and the two million other people in this quiet corner of the country were driving around in circles looking for a place to park.

Have you ever looked at people? I mean really looked at them! They are all different. Fat, slim, tall, short, pretty, ugly, and pretty ugly. They all look so bloody miserable. Joe Blow there, with his wife Mabel. Would have won fifty million on the lottery only his fecking stupid wife forgot to buy the ticket. Serves him right, that will teach him to come out walking on the same day as me.

There is a big sign on the lawn, it says; "It is forbidden to throw stones at this sign." There is another sign nearby, it says; FOR SALE . DES RES. CALL SIMON BEREBELLY AT SNOT, YATCH & WANKA, ESTATE AGENTS.

Or some thing like that. In the same garden there was yet another FOR SALE sign put there by FROSTY KNICKER & DOLITTLE

One house, two signs. Now why do they expect to sell the house twice? A good idea if you can get away with it!

# A CHAPTER ON WALES

Yes, a whole chapter on Wales .

My first visit to Wales was almost a disaster - for me, that is, not Wales .

It was beautiful. I drove through the morning mist into this valley in Llangollen. The sun was just breaking over the mountains (all Wales is mountains!) and the lights of the small town flickered through the struggling dawn. Birds were waking up and the odd blackbird swished dangerously close to the car as it crossed the road, flying just above the ground. I was so enthralled with the scene that I took my eyes off the road - a very dangerous thing to do in Wales , they don't drive cars, they aim them!

I stopped the car at the bridge, got out and walked over to the river. The roaring of the water was like a tonic. Heavy rain most of the preceding week had turned the usually turbulent river into a vast, heaving cauldron of sight, colour and sound. It was magnificent.

My wife sat huddled in the car, reluctant to leave the warmth and join me.

A policeman came over and stood beside me. "I have been living and working in this town for forty years – man and boy – and it never ceases to raise a lump in my throat." His accent was deep and sing-song, like a piece of music being recited. I love the Welsh accent

"I have to agree with you there, it is a sight to dream about."

We stood talking for about fifteen minutes when my wife joined us. "Is there a toilet around here?" she asked the policeman.

"No, not really. We have one but it doesn't open until 9 o'clock, but come with me back to the station, you can use the one there and I will put the kettle on." We joined him, and he did just that, even managing to make a bacon sandwich on the old cooker they had.

The Welsh are like that, they are a warm and friendly people – if they like you. Wales is the same, like it and the sun will shine; don't like it and it rains like shit all day long!

Wales is full of cliffs, high mountains and flowing rivers. The rain, which does fall often, even when it does like you, has to go somewhere, so it heads for the sea almost as soon as it hits the ground.

It is no earthly good trying to find your way around the country, all the signs are in Welsh. Just pick the road that looks the most attractive - with plenty of room for vehicles to pass you - and you will, eventually, find a nice place to stop.

Last time I was in Wales we stayed at a lovely sea side town called Colwyn Bay . It is one of those towns that could only exist in Wales . The bay it overlooks is picturesque.

Mountains - alright, hills, sweep down through the town onto the shore. Halfway down the hills the woods are thick with rhododendrons, multi-coloured and deeply set in the little valleys.

Out of season - that's when I like Colwyn Bay best, the town is quiet, almost sleeping. That is when you see the most interesting people. I love watching people.

My favourite character used to sit on a bench outside the station, the railroad station.

I never got to know his name, I just called him Dai.

Dai was about 75 or 80 years old. His clothes were clean, expensive-looking, but well worn. A cloth cap sat jauntily on his head, he pushed it back onto the crown of his grey covered, woolly hair and wiped his brow with a red hanky, which he carefully folded and put back into his pocket.

The hat brim was then pulled down over his forehead. He did this often, although the day was not that warm.

He sat on the wooden bench with one arm resting along the back, the other hand in his raincoat pocket. A smile gently rested on his mouth and in his eyes, a smile that said 'nothing is new; I've seen it all before, long ago when I was younger'. But I never got the impression that his smile was critical of the world around him. He just seemed contented.

Some days he would get up from the bench and wander the few hundred yards through the tunnel under the railroad track and down to the sandy beach, not far from the pier. There he had another bench, another favourite perch; he sat there in the same position, watching the ships, the sea gulls and the puffins – Puffin Island is not that far away, more towards Llandudno, a bigger seaside town.

Some days Dai would bring a sandwich, carefully wrapped in a brown paper bag. This he would eat slowly and methodically, throwing the crusts to the ever present, ever greedy gulls.

I made a point of getting up in the mornings, leaving the wife still asleep in bed, and wandering down to look for Dai. His favourite time – except on the one day it rained, it was 8 o-clock. He would do his sitting and rambling between 8 and 9 am. What he did during the rest of the time I never found out.

I got the urge to speak to him, to find out just who he was and what wonderful secrets he held stored in his mind, and his heart. We all have stories to tell.

What, or who, was Dai? An old soldier? A farmer, now retired? A banker, bricklayer, baker, coalman? Or was he just an old man who had lived his life and now wanted to watch other people live theirs.

My favourite poem is Thomas Gray's Elegy Written in a Country Church Yard. He too watched people; he watched the ploughman making his way back to the farm - with the horses , at the end of a days work.

"The curfew tolls the knell of passing day.
The lowing herd wind slowly o'er the lea,
The plowman homeward plods his weary way,
And leaves the world to darkness and to me."

This really is the most beautiful poem ever written. It is Life, it is about Life. It is about people.

On the last day we stayed in Colwyn Bay I got up early and went out to see 'Dai'; he wasn't there. I hurried down to the beach - no little old man on the bench.

I was devastated, what could have happened to him? I decided to walk quickly around the block. Just in case he had overslept, or maybe found another place to sit and watch the world. Eventually I found him. He was sitting in the window of a tea room. Newspaper in front of him, and a cup of tea which he thoughtfully stirred with the spoon. On an impulse I decided to make myself known to this lovely old man who had fascinated me over the past week.

I entered the café and walked over to his table.

"Excuse me, sorry to bother you, but I couldn't help noticing you weren't in your usual place - you know, on the bench by the station, this morning."

He looked up at me and smiled, his carefully shaven face full of freshness, and determination shone in his eyes –' here was a man' I said to myself, 'who is contented with his life; whose courage and endurance had seen the worst that the world could throw at him, and has remained with dignity and forbearance. One of life's gentlemen.'

Without losing that smile, the smile of a patient man who believed he had encountered the world's best idiot, he replied;

"No, not this morning, too f...ing cold!"

# A CHAPTER ON MERVIN ELLIOT

The last time I saw Merv he was forty years old, balding, and very overweight - something that he always said he would do something about. But, being Merv, he never did. The first time I ever saw Merv I was about six and he weren't much older or younger. Either way, he would still have been Merv.

His full name was Mervin Elliot and he lived on a farm in Scotland Ontario. Merv was a good mate of mine and we spent many years being friends. We also spent many years not really caring about where we both were or what we were doing.

During the times when we were in contact with each other we appeared to have a lot of fun. We played ice hockey, sometimes on the same team and sometimes on different teams - regardless of which ever it was, for or against, we would always try and kill each other. Merv was bigger and heavier than me, but I was faster than he. I still managed to get hurt quite often.

Merv was an untidy sod. He combed his hair only when he had a date with a girl (about twice a year) and he wore the same clothes to go drinking in that he wore to do the milking. That way there was never any doubt in people's minds as to what Merv did for a living. He stank of cow shit all the time - unless, of course, he ran over a skunk then he stank of skunk -which is pretty bloody awful.

We had quick and messy cure for skunk smell - tomato juice. We bought it from the store for about 38 cents a can, and, when the need arose, we splashed the tomato juice all over the 'skunked' part - either us or the car we had run over the little bastard with. If you have to douse yourself with tomato juice you then found a lake, pond or river and jumped in until juice and skunk has washed off. All you then have to worry about was drying off!

Skunks were shit - unless you were a female skunk, that is.

Merv was smarter than me, he went to college. OK, I went to college as well, but Merv paid attention in the class room, I looked around to see what was on offer from the female fraternity.

Merv wound up with a BSc at the University of Southern Ontario and I wound up playing yet another season up in the boondocks for a team that could hardly afford to keep the ice cold yet alone pay us a wage! Still, it was fun.

Merv had a pretty little wife called Maureen. She was half his weight, half his height and twice as smart. She had a temper like there was no tomorrow, and let fly at Merv any time she crossed him. "Get the hell out of here, you lazy, good for nothing!" she would whisper to him, and he would do just whatever she told him - firmly in the belief that she was only joking - I was never of the opinion one way or t'other - I, being a devout coward, stayed well out of it!

Merv had a weakness, well, some may even call it a problem, Merv enjoyed a good fart.

It made no earthly difference to Merv where he was or who he was with, if Merv wanted to fart, Mervin farted. It could be in the most sad part of Love Story - where the girl is doing the dying bit - an extra loud fart here, which brought the house to a state of hilarious uproar - and the usherette running down the stairs with her flashlight, and had every one pointing at every one else and saying, "it was her - or him".

Merv even farted at his mother's funeral - yes, during the sad bit, but his excuse for that was, "so that she will know I'm here."

He may have had a point there; no one else could fart like Merv.

Hearing that fart, his mother would know that he was alright.

Just watched a programme on the old telly, this was about a chap who had just written a book about some feller who had written a book about a bird that some naturalist had painted a picture about some two hundred years ago. No one has ever seen the bird since then, but the Natural History Museum had actually accepted the fact that this bird existed! Come on!

OK, so I will paint a picture about this six foot mouse – with horns and a ten foot tail that lives down the bottom of my garden. I am the only one to see it and I have only seen it once and I will probably never see it again. I will send a copy of the painting to the Natural History Museum and I fully expect some feller to write a book about me and the mouse. OK?

Merv had the idea that he could live forever. He worked out that if one was to avoid all the things that would and could kill you, then you would not die.

He ate only good, healthy food, lots of salads, lots of fruit, no burgers, no coke, no alcohol other than red wine and the occasional Scotch whisky. He exercised regularly and only made love to his wife if there was a Wednesday in the week.

Merv never flew and never went further out in a boat than he could swim back easily.

Merv made it to 63.

Merv's calculations had failed to take in the 18-wheeler whose brakes failed on Highway 2, and crushed him and the car he was driving.

I miss Merv, he was such a laugh.

## ANOTHER CHAPTER

### ON SOMETHING ELSE

Growing old is pure crap, don't let any one tell you different. You look back on everything and realise that it is beyond your grasp. The only things that you can do when you are old that you did when you were young are eat, drink, sleep and shit. And sometimes those things don't always work out!

It's like an old bull, two days away from the butchers slab, looking at a herd of cows - and dreaming!

Well I've done my share of dreaming.

Dreams are funny things, Disney summed it up with the best description I have ever heard when he said "dreams are a wish your heart makes", that's pretty good, and it really hits the nail right on the nose! Think about it.

I used to dream a lot when I was a kid, now I dream most of the time. It's great, in dreams you can skate faster, drive quicker and newer cars, climb mountains, drink crates of Scotch, travel the world - free, and make love all night! Now that really is something!

Then there are the people you meet in dreams, most of them are people you know, but in dreams they are different, funnier, wilder, happier, more willing to join you in your mad escapades, almost as if they knew they were sharing your dream and wish the dream could come true. What if that was possible? What if the dreams were really the reality and what we believe is the life we are living is really the dream? Think about it; just think of the possibilities that open up?

Then there is space. Saw a programme last night about space. Apparently only 4 per cent of space is occupied, the other 96% is empty. That's an awful lot of room. Time, now there's something else connected with space. We don't really know what time is, do we; I mean we invented time just to fill the hours of night and day. Time is a figment of our imagination. Maybe space is as well. It is possible that the universe, all the millions- billions of years since the 'big bang' are really just a moment or two in someone else's time. Like suppose a really big 'Being' dropped a tear and that tear was the universe and all the stars and all the things and all the people in it, and suppose that the time the tear dropped from the 'Beings' eye until it hit the floor was the billions of years in our time, think about it! Time is relative, so Einstein said, time is relative to us because we are experiencing it, but if someone else was experiencing it then it would not be governed by the same rules as we know!

Maybe the universe is so infinitely small that billions of them could sit on the head of a pin. Maybe the millions of years that man has been around only amounted to the time it takes a flash of lightening to hit the ground.

I am five foot eight, but only because we measure things against the things we know, mountains, trees, etc., shit I may only be minus an inch to the power of ten - now that is really small.

Trouble is, we just don't know, we have no idea just how big space is or how long time it. IF a spaceman travelled millions of miles at the speed of light and then came back to earth he would have aged the time he took to travel (at the speed of light), but when he got back to earth hundreds of years would have passed.

Something like going to town and back on the train!

I would love to go back in time and look at the wonderful old people and things, the wonderful towns and villages - only some of the things in the past I would not like, I know that, the poverty, decease, etc.

I don't think we will ever travel forward in time, I mean you can't go to something, somewhere that hasn't existed yet, can you?, and if something has not happened then it doesn't exist, and the moment you got there anyway it would not be the future, it would be the present, and a second later it would be the past. Follow me? No? not too sure I follow me either!

# BECAUSE IT IS THERE!

## AN HEROIC CHAPTER

Because it is there! The reasons why people climb mountains, swim oceans, get married! Etc. It is probably also the feeblest excuse anyone had to do anything.

"Why did you rob that bank, you villain?"

"Because it was there, your honour."

"Why did you rape that pretty young maiden, you fiend?"

"Because she was there your worship".

"Why did you drive into that parked car, you imbecile?"

"Because it was there, guv."

See what I mean? THE most stupid excuse for anything.

We can't just go around climbing things because they are there; it is too ridiculous for words. Suppose we all went around climbing things 'because they are there'? See what I mean?

The world is full of mountains, and full of water - lakes, oceans, rivers, and if we all took it upon ourselves to climb and swim everything where would it end?

Why don't we all go off and do something useful, like finishing off the Great Wall of China, or Hadrian's Wall - neither one is finished yet. Then there is the rain forest in Brazil to be re-planted,, or all the rubbish collected from the base camps on Everest, a few buckets of water in the Australian outback would be handy, I mean there is simply a host of things to do that are useful, climbing a mountain just is not useful, it accomplished nothing, going up Everest. And why swim the Channel, ships, boats and planes go across it all-day long, they've even built a tunnel under it - why swim the damned thing?

The way I figure it we do too many unnecessary things - like why iron the backs of shirts, or sheets - other than the bit you fold over the blanket at the top. Or pruning trees and bushes - they only grow back! You don't see God, or Mother Nature walking around the forest hacking off branches, do you? So why do we bother?

I don't need a haircut, I don't need so many buttons on my shirt, I don't need to kiss Aunt Bertha (cousin Paddy was OK though!)

And when you think about it, Everest is 29,031 feet tall at this moment; 20,000,000 years ago it was only about ten foot tall - now that would have been the best time to climb it. Wouldn't have needed Sherpa Tensing, or oxygen, or all that warm clothing, they could have saved a fortune!

The other night I dreamed I was walking through a strange town. It was full of strange people, millions of them, all pushing and shoving, all in a hurry to get nowhere fast. I felt I couldn't breath, they were all using up the air and there was none left for me. I wanted to kill all the other people, I hated them, but I didn't kill them. I wanted to grab all the air and keep it to myself. Then in my dream I walked around a corner in the town and the wind was blowing - too much fecking air now.

# A 'LONG AGO' CHAPTER

When I was a kid, long, long ago, we lived on a farm not far from the Six Nations Indian Reservation, Brantford. Being close to the Indians, we more or less grew up with the kids. I had a good friend, a close friend, a very pretty girl with long, dark hair and, like all the girls I knew, big tits. Her granddad was a real character.

Elaine was quietly spoken, gently and lovely. I was bewitched by her. Most of the bewitchment came from the fact that at that age I was hugely influenced on my outlook on life by the cinema. We didn't have viable TV then and had to rely on the movie – mostly Saturday matinee which had a very restricted curriculum consisting of Cowboy and Indians, Science Fiction – Buck Rodgers, Superman, etc., Cops and Robbers, and comedy, the Marks Brothers, The Three Stooges, Laurel and Hardy etc. We saw Cowboy and Indian films because they were mostly believable! I, being young and really stupid used to talk to Elaine's granddad and ask him really stupid questions about whether or not he had ever fought against Custer – he used to really take the piss and lead me on about his exploits – though Elaine did tell me that he would probably kill himself with a bow and arrow, and that the nearest he ever came to a horse was at the race track!.

He used to say to me, "I'm going out to the woods this weekend to learn how to be an Indian again, gonna scalp a few white men and drink a lot of whisky." Well he did drink a lot of whisky, Indians, after about 1951 were allowed to drink and they could cross the border into the US without restriction, and as soon as they got their cheque from the government they would go across the border and get tanked up. Poor sods, after the government took everything away from them they had precious little left.

I never did find out what her granddad's real name was, I suppose it was because I wasn't really interested. He told me lots of strange names, and I guess he just forgot what he'd told me the first time round. Sometimes he was chief Wonky Horse, other times it was chief Broken Lance, or chief Tellbigstory - never knew, never cared, he was a wonderful old man and I suppose I just felt sorry for him. Elaine didn't want to spoil his dream so she wouldn't tell me.

He died about two years after I stopped seeing her, and I like to think of him as my 'real Indian friend', he was all of that. I often wondered if maybe he was really a warrior when he was young – he must have been old enough to have ridden with Crazy Horse, or Yellow Hands. Anyhow, I will never know now.

Got to thinking the other day, 'bout all this replacement stuff.

They can give you new kidneys, new hearts, new liver, new faces, new legs, arms etc., even new willies, so if I live till I'm about 90 I can get all the bits replaced and start all over again! Fantastic! Just think of it, another 90 years then have all the bits replaced again, feck, you can live forever! And feck forever! If they keep giving you new willies and balls. OK, I'm sold, when do we start?

Only thing is I just don't trust doctors and surgeons, I mean all those sick people going into hospitals and coming out worse – or dead – which is worse. Doctors train for only four years, veterinarian surgeons train for seven – I think if I get anything done I will go to the vet – safer!

## WALK INTO YOUR MIND!

### A CHAPTER GOING NOWHERE!

Do just that - walk into your mind. Explore the darkest, deepest reaches of your inner most thoughts; look for the things hidden in the recess, the nooks and crannies of your thoughts, dreams, and aspirations. Look as far as you can into places unvisited or forgotten. Tell me what you find. Look into the attic where all your dreams are stored, some recalled, some forgotten forever, and some just waiting for you to stir them into every day use again.

Memories are good, though some are bad. Some are best forgotten, and it is these 'best forgotten' memories that you need to drag out and investigate, look at them really hard, and see if maybe there is some room for reconciliation, some leeway that you could extend to the thoughts you cast aside. It is much like putting an old jacket into the cupboard, discarding it, then, months or years later finding it again and realising that once it was a much loved and cared about thing that gave you comfort and warmth, and that maybe you should put it on again - and enjoy it.

It is like that with the things we cast aside in our minds.

In the Windmills of your mind – a very beautiful song that was feature in the first version of the Thomas Crown Affair, contains some lovely words – 'why did summer go so quickly, was it something that I said', 'keys that jingle in your pocket, thoughts that jangle in your head,' it goes on, and on. And it is so true.

Thoughts catch up with us. You can never get them out of your mind, they are there, and they haunt you, day and night.

The things that happen to you in the daylight hours tiptoe gently through your mind during the wee small hours, invading your dreams, always there, always.

Sit on a crowded train, or walk through a leafy wood; stand alone on a windy hill, or drive through a motorway of traffic; the thoughts are there. You will recall something said, something done; something unkindly said, or a good deed done. Some thoughts will bring a tear to your eye, others make you weep with shame, but they are there, just below the surface.

Ever see a man sitting alone on a park bench, or along the sea wall on the promenade; ever see a farm worker stop the plough and look far off across the meadows. Ever see a lonely old man standing silently at attention in the military cemetery, gazing at the aged, moss-strewn cross, with a tear in his eye. You could not afford to buy his memories, they are too precious.

I often saw my old granny sitting in her rocking chair, glasses held loosely in her hand, knitting resting on her lap, eyes wide open. "Penny for your thoughts, Gran." I would say to her.

"Oh, just biding my time, just biding my time." She would reply.

It took me forty years to understand what she meant.

Day-dreaming, some call it. Living in the past – as others would say. Living again, is the true name for it, living among the folks, the times, the laughter, the tears, the joy, the sorrow, and the many other things that go to make a life worth living.

# A CHAPTER ON ANGELS

Way back in the early nineteen fifties I told Andy Kaupi that he had a Guardian Angel.

"Fuck off; what would I want with a guardian angel?" Was his immediate and well thought out reply.

"We all have them Andy, every one of us."

"Well it didn't do that f...ing rabbit any good, did it, just shot its f...ing balls off."

Andy spoke like that most of the time. His mother - or his father, was a throwback from the time before man learned to stand upright and hold a spoon when he drank soup.

Nevertheless, Andy was a star hockey player and one of the best centre ice players I have ever been on the wing with, could he skate!

Andy was not very big, only about five nine, and weighed in at just over 140 pounds, but he could move like greased lightning.

But he swore all the time, on the ice or off it.

Any way, this guardian angel thing. "No kidding Andy, we all have them except animals - well, OK, so no one knows, maybe animals have them as well, don't really know about that one, but I do know you have one, watches over you all the time."

Andy looked over his shoulder across the snow-covered field.

"So where is this f...ing angel then?"

Andy was nervous, I could tell that. He didn't really know whether to believe me or not, but weighed against that was the fact that I had never lied to or tricked Andy and he had no reason not to believe me - after all I had been to college whereas Andy hadn't even graduated from kindergarten, let alone grade school.

"Oh, you can't see them, but believe me they are there, all the time. They watch over you and try to help you and things."

"Well yes, you may have something there; I did score four goals last week against the Lions."

" Well I don't know if that is the kind of help they are supposed to give you, I mean spiritual help, like look after your conscience, help you make the right decision, and things like that. Maybe save you from danger - you know, like that time you didn't want to drive over that snow-covered bridge, and then we found it weren't there."

"Oh, yeah, see what you mean, yeah, you could be right, hell, never thought of that."

He looked aver his shoulder again and, for good measure, looked up at the sky as well.

"What do you reckon mine is a feller or a gal, or maybe some relative like my Granny?"

"Yep, that is possible, could be your Granny – when did she die – how long ago?"

"Hell, no, Granny is still alive, but she always fussed over me when I went to see her."

I looked at this poor, lost soul and realised that maybe I had opened a can of worms that would have been better left closed up.

"Not quite like that Andy, Angels are mostly people in our past, ones who have been assigned to look after us, you know, like they used to tell us when we went to Sunday school".

"Know what you mean, but I only ever went to Sunday school once, fell asleep and got kicked out."

About this time I started wishing that another rabbit would run from cover and give Andy something else to think about, but just my luck, it started to snow again, quite heavily.

# CHASING CHICKENS

## A CHAPTER OF REVELATION

On a farm, and, probably, not on a farm, the most dead-end job in the world is chasing chickens. Why do I say that? Simple, when I was a kid, on the farm, at Christmas time - and any other time that we felt hungry and wanted to eat something, my job was to catch the food. Chickens, because they are small and very quick, are probably the hardest things to catch, me, being too young to bump off said food, had the odious job of catching the fecking things! Thus, chasing chickens becomes the bottom of the heap, last step on the ladder, the KRAP job.

Now I am not saying that the above statement is true on all accounts, there may well be people out there who really enjoy chasing chickens. In fact I knew a chap once, in Sudbury, Suffolk, who chased chickens for a living, he enjoyed, was reasonably well paid, and adopted an affinity with the birds. BUT, given the choice of occupations/jobs, my leanings would be towards NOT chasing chickens. Just thought I would make the point!

It would also help a lot if you had the chickens in a small, enclosed, area. Chasing the fecking things around a forty-acre field is way out. Another bad place to chase chickens is in a wood or forest. Chickens have wings, and although they can not fly very high or very far, the buggers can flutter quite high up in trees, and into brambles and other sneaky, hidey places. Chickens, one must assume, hate like feck getting caught!

But then chasing any kind of bird other than a Dodo (and that is exactly why we have no Dodo's, they couldn't and didn't run away and all got caught and eaten!) is not the easiest job in the world.

"Look son, all I want you to do is go out into the Serengeti and catch an ostrich for dinner, OK?"

Like feck!

Turkey and geese were bad enough; anything else would have been right out of the question!

The point I am trying to make is that a lot of jobs are really necessary, however lowly and underpaid or uninteresting they may seem some poor sod has to do them. No chaser, no chicken, no chicken, no eats!

It's a bummer, but that's life for you, some arsehole always gets stuck with the wrong end of the mule!

My other job was digging up worms. I used to like fishing, but in order to go fishing with my sister's boyfriend I had to dig the worms, and I hate worms, fecking awful things!

Climbing trees is another useful skill to have - especially if you have a job chasing chickens, and they are in the woods.

Some trees just beg to be climbed. I remember once we had two Cedars of Lebanon, beautiful trees, elegant, stately, and magnificent, branches that spread out over the garden, sheltering us from the sun and playing host to more birds than you could shake a stick at. They had a big problem though; they were virtually un-climbable - well to me, that is. I can climb most trees - well, when I was a lot younger - but cedars were not that easy, even if you tried it you got covered in gum that was almost impossible to wash off!

It was very easy to adopt a tree. Most country kids have favourite, a tree that they love to climb and sit among the branches. You can imagine all kinds of things when sitting in a tree.

I often used to get my brothers to build me a tree house, or at least a platform, that way if you fell asleep you wouldn't fall off!

# A CHAPTER ON

## PAIN THAT MAKES OTHER MEN THINK

The other evening I watched Andrea Bocceli sing, in case his name means nothing to you, he is the blind tenor who sings the classics and, occasionally, more 'pop' music. His voice is inspired, it also makes that little tingle up and down you spine when you realise that the man with the voice is unable to see the world around him. That is really spooky.

Many years ago I suffered a blow to my head that gave me a loss of sight for a few days, luckily, I regained my sight (none of my sense other than that!) Andre never will, not unless some absolute miracle comes along.

Not being able to see anything is scary. Just think about it. All around you are things happening, little things, car horns, revving engines, people shouting (your hearing, sometimes, is much more acute when you lose your sight) bangs, whistles, clashes, crashes, NOISE; and then there are other sounds, birds singing, the wind in the trees, the meowing of cats, the bark of dogs, the cry of a baby, the question of a child. You hear the gently cry of a lost soul, or a tearful lover. And that is all you know about them, the sound.

You don't know the reason behind the sound. You don't know where the car is coming from, why the child is weeping. You cannot tell whether the singing bird is blue, green, brown or black. You don't even know if the wind has colour.

And that is weird.

To love some one, or, like Andrea, stand along side a girl like Katherine and know whether or not she is beautiful. To know what 'beautiful' looks like; to be able to envisage a lovely face, a beautiful face, without ever having seen one. Yes, he knows what the voice is like, he understands that her voice is beautiful, but to put a picture to that face is something he cannot do.

That is scary.

How do you describe a tree to someone who has never seen one? Try it.

Sight is the one thing that we tend to take for granted - until we lose it. But even if you lose your sight after having been able to see is better than never seeing at all.

That is another thing I shall have to take up with the Big Feller when I see Him. To deprive some one of the right to see this crazy, lovely world is not justice, it is downright cruel. Even saying that Bocelli may not have developed his beautiful voice if he could see is no answer. It is just that, downright cruel - especially for an omnipotent God.

But then again, do we have the freedom of choice? If we are made in God's image then surely that makes us as God in many ways, therefore, if we are made in His image, we have all His powers - and His weaknesses. Or are we just made in His image from the physical appearance?

We are, or we are not. There can be no half-way thing. Make us as you, and we are as one.

Must we obey the dictates that our origins would suggest?

For a start we do not have God's powers - I don't, anyway. Nor would I want them!

There are many questions, too many, and for this frail little mind, questions need answers. Maybe that is the whole secret of life, to have us forever seeking the answers to questions that we may never find the answer.

But that will not help Andrea Bocceli and the other talented, sadly handicapped men and women of genius who give us so much in the form of beauty, and who have lost so much themselves.

Some of life's mysteries really suck. Why can we not all be content and happy. Why must we have to suffer? OK, so suffering teaches, pain makes man think, thought makes man wise, wisdom makes life more endurable. That concept is OK for grown adults, they who have found a place in life,; who have tasted the fruit and then want to improve or change, but what about the others, too young and too innocent to ever have known Life? Is suffering and pain a fair trial to put them through?

I doubt it.

# A CHAPTER ON COOKING

I have a cousin. In order to avoid any embarrassment to him (he is still alive, well and kicking!), I will not use his real name, Colin, I will call him Fred instead.

Fred neither is nor was renowned for his culinary skills. He was very skilful at many other things, but culinary skills were definitely not one of them.

I first found this out when a few friends of ours – including myself – went round to our aunt's place one weekend in order to decorate it while she was away. Fred had the task of feeding us with a roast beef dinner which he proceeded to cook while we all mucked in with the decorating.

Eventually, about midday someone mentioned lunch and the fact that the pubs closed at 2 pm in almost the same breath.

"OK," said Fred, I will shove the grub in oven and we will go across the road to the pub for an hour – which we all did.

Well over an hour later we returned from the pub and got stuck into the work again. Fred said the meat was ready and he then put the potatoes on. An hour later the potatoes were done so he then put the vegetables on. When the vegetables were done he made the gravy. By this time the meat was stone cold and the potatoes were heading in the same direction.

I have never had a cold roast dinner before – or since.

Fred was undeterred, he then made a trifle using the instructions he found in a cook book. The whole thing finally set two days after our aunt returned.

We never got to eat it – which was probably just as well.

This got me thinking, just why do we eat food the way we do? We have a starter, then a fish course (in posh places anyhow) and a main course followed by a desert – usually something sweet. Why?

Why not mix the whole lot together on the same plate – why not have roast turkey and trifle, or roast pork and rice pudding, or steak and blancmange? Even fish and chocolate cheesecake? Think about it, you have probably eaten much worse, especially if you visit fast-food burger joints!

Animals aren't that fussy, pigs will eat anything in any order, I know, we used to keep pigs on the farm; they will get stuck in to anything!

Think of the time it would save - especially in busy restaurants, instead of bringing several different dishes spread out over the evening, they could bring the whole lot together, on one plate, and then bugger off for the rest of the night!

Same with the drinks, it is possible to have as many as eight different glasses in front of you in some of the posh restaurants - all you really need is a pint mug, bung the whole lot into it, and enjoy yourself! OK, so you may have to keep the coffee separate, but that still cuts down the amount of sand they have to turn into glasses in the factory! Less glass - more beaches!

Think of all the washing up you would save, less washing up - less water used! Got to be good for the environment if nothing else!

It may even help your digestive system, just think of all the re-adjustments the old gut has to make every now and then:

'coming down - one dollop of hot soup!'

'Get ready, here comes the fish course!'

'Back on your feet, ice cream and jelly on its way!'

'Hold fire, big, big chunk of Gorgonzola and biscuits heading your way!'

# CHAPTER TO THINK ABOUT…

IF a tree were to fall down in the forest, and no one was there to hear it, would it make a noise? The answer is NO. IF there were one to hear it would not be a noise, it would make a sound; and as a 'sound' it can only exist IF some one hears it! Therefore, the answer is simply, NO.

The simple definition of sound - as found in most dictionaries, explains that sound, noise etc. is made by vibrations through the air as a result of something happening to trigger these 'vibrations', the result only becomes a 'sound', or a 'noise' if someone hears it. No person ergo, no sound or noise.

Now you may say to yourselves, "What is he on about"? and you may say that with some justification, mainly because I am never very sure just what I am on about at any time - however, the object is to stimulate your brain cells and make you think about the things I put forward - or some of them, anyway.!

Another point that needs clearing up. It is all very well to tell us that only 4% of the known universe contains any matter (things like stars, worlds, planets, flying saucers etc.) what about our oceans? We know more about the dark side of the moon than we do about that bloody big puddle that fills up the spaces between England, America, Australia, New Zealand, Greenland and Lower Slobbovia . All we know is that it is wet, salty, full of things that can be eaten and will, just as happily, eat you, and that ships will float on it most of the time, though quite often they don't float. Some of them intentionally sail below the surface, and some more often don't float as well as we would like to hope - the Titanic being a specific example, and the Tirpitz another one - not to mention the fecking rowing boat I got into down on the river once!

Now the point I am attempting to get at is this; we spend the first nine months of your lives floating and living quite happily in water. Then the day arrives when we are kicked out into the cruel world and have to learn - quickly - how to breathe air! No warning, no time to figure it out, and if, the second you are expelled into the cold, noisy, room, IF you don't immediately start sucking air some arsehole gives you an almighty whack on your bum, to make you cry! Well. It would, wouldn't it?

From that moment on, should we decide that we would like to go back to living in water, we can't. The second we do - we drown! How fecking stupid is that?

Would it not make a lot more sense if we were able to breathe both water and air? We could then live under water some of the time, play with the dolphins, catch and eat really fresh fish, and in the bargain, we would have a lot more room to move around in!

Now it shouldn't take too much effort for all those clever types in the laboratories to figure out a way to get us breathing in and out of water. This could be the next major project for Science, much more sensible than trying to get cars to run on peanut oil, or piss and vinegar, or whatever!

Think about it! You know it makes sense.

All those whales that we like to kill and eat - and sharks - well it would be an equal playing field, would it not! If you throw a harpoon at a fecking big whale and miss - you had better learn to swim really, really fast!

Also it would make it a lot easier to look around those old wrecks laying down there, must be a fortune in gold and silver just lying on the sea bed, waiting for you to pick it up.

# HISTORY

## A CHAPTER ABOUT OLD THINGS

It would appear that Judas is no longer to be regarded as a betraying son of a bitch. Recent finds show that he is, in fact, a conspirator who only did Jesus' bidding. Jesus actually wanted the crucifixion to take place. No one is completely certain of his motives. Maybe it was the ultimate Grand Design. I just wish, for Judas' sake, He had left a note some where that absolved Judas from all blame. I mean it just ain't fair that the poor sod should spend 2,000 years in purgatory for a crime he didn't commit. Had it happened today he would have been awarded about fifty million quid in compensation!

But then history is like that, too many wrongs, too many rights, too little understanding.

Another thing, Can anyone give me a valid reason just why the Queen and her ilk should feel themselves to be better, and above any other person in this country? A couple of hundred years ago all the royal family won their spurs on the field of battle, how come the Queen and all the other hangers-on don't have to get out there and slug it out with the opposition?

Maybe that is the trouble with the country today, too many people living off the past glory - like a shop or restaurant with a good reputation that cannot find the will to keep up the effort.

Scrap the lot and start again, from the bottom this time!

There was a time, several hundred years ago, when kings and the like were real men. They fought on the battlefields of history, shaping the countries, the lands, towns, villages and the people into what we find today. Some of these men were right villains, bullies and tyrants; some were good, well-meaning, honest men. Most of the historical facts have been distorted by a lack of reading and writing; a lack of records that meant most things were passed down in the form of stories - and any one knows, tell a man a story (or, better still, tell a woman a story!) and the damn thing will change several times in the first three "telling's!"

For all we know, King Arthur, with all his knights of the round table, really did exist and was a good man, a man of integrity and a man of honour. He must have been some real type of man to have done just a half the deeds he was credited with, but nonetheless, good Arthur stands very high in my book. So much so that I think it is high time we put him up for sainthood and put firmly in place of that upstart Saint George who was nothing more than a Turk who got caught up in the Roman Legion and never even came to Britain! Who put him up for sainthood?

No, it has to be Arthur and his very shaggable Guinevere, (even if old Lancelot – that two-timing frog, did get his leg over the poor damsel.

It is all very well to tell a story and get it believed. If it is plausible then, regardless of the bits and pieces around the edges, people will believe it.

It is like that fantastic scene in Father Ted where he, Ted, gets stuck with the forfeit and has to kick Bishop Brennan up the arse. He decides eventually that the only way to do it is just to kick his arse and look as if nothing has happened, and, sure enough, the Bishop, although he knows it has happened, finds it too incredible to believe, and just thinks he must have imagined it! Fantastic! And if I ever get that close to a Bishop…

I nearly did once; I was in a toilet in the Hotel Mount Royal in Montreal. There was a convention going on and I, having just played and lost a game with a Quebec 'B' team, was pissed out of my mind. I had just thrown up in the loo and was headed for the wash basin. Leaning over it was a man in a dark suit. "Can't get near the fucking bar in this place", I said to the man, "too full of fucking priests".

He stood up, taking a paper towel to dry his face, and I saw his collar.

Straight round the church the next morning, 16 'Hail Mary's, and fifty 'Our Fathers', before breakfast!

But there, I am distracted again. This is supposed to be a chapter about history!

History repeats itself. There are very few things that don't crop up time and time again. That is because people forget. Churchill said England was a nation of short memories. I know he meant it in a different context - he was talking about how he got bounced out of office after just saving the country from the Nazis, but he could have applied it to the people in general.

I have never come across such a lot of people with very, very short memories. We can go a whole winter without a day of rain, then it rains, on and off, for two days. The first person you meet will say, "Will it never stop raining?"

And if they owe you money - forget it! They will!

It is little wonder that history is so inaccurate!

We often visit old castles and things (well, you can't really have a 'new' castle, can you?), anyway, these old places, wonderful as they are, always leave me with slight bewilderment - the item of bewilderment being the castle 'loo'.

Very simple in construction, they usually consist of just a small room with a hole in the wall that drops straight down into the moat below - fantastic! It really is something from the past that should have been continued into the present day! I would love to have one of these things in my house - right over the front door! Just think of the benefits - ring, ring, Jehovah Witnesses, or Insurance Salesman!

"Just stand there for a minute, be right with you! Now look up!"

Just brilliant! Modern toilets all that waste of shit!

I am going to look up my builder's number right now...

Another thing that history can teach us is the drawbridge, now why on earth did we ever stop putting them on houses? It is the perfect way to discourage visitors, stop burglars and make it very difficult for the 'outlaws' to come and visit. You could also fish in it.

We visit a lot of places, the wife and I. We go to these great big country estates and walk around all day taking hundreds of pictures. We have tea and cake in the café, pee in the toilets, and buy the odd souvenir plant or ornament.

The pictures stay in the camera for several months until we have safely forgotten where we were when we took them; the souvenirs get left in the car until we trade it in, and the plants all die before we get home. This is because we always visit these places in the hot summer weather and forget to water the plants.

This is something we do every summer; we are getting quite good at it now.

Our children keep telling us to get a life.

The other thing we like to do is drive hundreds of miles into the West Country, or Yorkshire, or Wales, or Kent, or the Cotswolds. When we get there we stay in relatively cheap but nice hotels where we immediately shower for at least an hour (using all their hot water and clean towels) then we go out in search of food, unless the hotel has a dining room. If it doesn't then we book a table and go out and have a 'Chinese' just down the road.

My wife likes to have at least two pillows so I spend half an hour wandering around the hotel trying to find someone who speaks English so that I can ask them for another pillow. This invariably has me wandering past the bar and, invariably, the barmaid has a French accent and big tits. I have never been known to pass up a barmaid with a French accent and ANY size tits so I always stop and have a whisky - or two. When this happens I then don't want to drive so we stay in and eat at the restaurant at which we have already booked!

The other thing we like to do in these hotels is order papers for the next morning. It is fun. You go up to the reception desk and ask the young lady for morning papers. She struggles with her English and the comprehension regarding papers in the morning. After she has promised that the chambermaid will take some up to your room immediately, you finally get her to understand what you really want. So you order the Mail and the Express. The real fun starts in the morning when you find either the Sun, the Times or the Evening Standard sent up from Hastings .

The best hotels are really the ones that are situated next door to a burger bar - you get very little choice of a meal, the drinks come in a machine and you speak to no one other than a sweet little thing who didn't even know you were coming (you are bloody lucky we have a cancellation mate!) and since you paid into their website a week ago, no further conversation is needed!

I also like to find pubs with exotic menus and really quaint dining rooms, and fifty different types of malt whisky, so that when I get back home I can tell this friend of mine (who likes to eat out, and will travel hundreds of miles on my recommendation!) about this fantastic pub up in the North Riding of Yorkshire that is on top of this really high hill, through a farmer's yard, a field of corn, a wood, and a swamp, and when you get there the dogs won't let you out of the car until you have thrown them a dead rabbit (that you have studiously run over and stopped to pick up in the farmer's field!)

I just love it when he comes back from a three week tour and tells me he couldn't find it. That's when I show him the brochure with the map printed on the back complete with instructions on how to get there.

My teacher always said I had a real mean streak – a bit of a bastard really- the teacher, not me!

## A CHAPTER ON THINGS

I have just read an article in a magazine about the threat to the World by global warming, a map of England shows a skeletal shape with just the mountains and bigger hills left habitable.

Think about it all you who spend your free time climbing. The World Is Yours!

And all you poor sods who have been ridiculed by your neighbours for building a boat in your back garden.

"How is he going to get that out of there?"

You are going to have the last laugh!

I am worried; never a strong swimmer I always had a tendency to sink – quickly! I liked my water either solidly frozen or in whisky!

I remember, as a child, all the doom and despondency that a select few spread around the globe. Personally, I don't believe it!

However, just suppose that I am wrong, now is the time to invest, heavily, in lifejackets and rowing boats. You never know!

It will have some advantages, instead of having to make long, expensive, overland treks to get to Everest in order to ascend the summit; you can sail right up to the first base camp and step ashore! Or wait until the whole fecking thing is almost under water, and build a house on top of it.

There is a strong belief held by many that we didn't evolve from the ape, or any other four or two-legged critter, but rather we evolved out of a sea creature - The Naked Dolphin was put forward as a stronger, more practical evolvement than the Naked Ape theory of Desmond Morris. We do have an awful lot in common with the dolphin - as we do with the ape, somehow, given the choice, I would rather have a dolphin for an ancestor than an ape! Wouldn't you?

And speaking of ancestors - and since, according to the experts, we are all descended from the one single family, how will it all end? Will we all evolve back into just one family, one little old woman living in darkest Africa? Will we all die out, move on, lose the use of all our bodies except our brain (that lets me out!) and this one, quivering mass of jelly - the last human being - sit gasping in the sun, unable to get a drink or a meal because the second from last servant kicked the bucket some days back. Is this how it will all end for us? Or will we head off into the stars in a rocket ship fuelled by lumps of sugar from the British Sugar Corporation?

IF, and it is an almighty big IF, Prof. Stephen Hawkin is right and Time, after the Universe has fully expanded, runs backwards, then we will, almost certainly, wind up as a little old lady in darkest Africa, whether or not we retain our bodies remains (some 500,000,000,000 years from now) to be seen. I won't be hanging around!

Now just think about that, suppose that in 500,000,000,000 years time you approach tomorrow - backwards! Everything you do that day you will have done before, years ago, but you are now going to do it backwards! Just think about it, the mind boggles. Pick the day's routine, each and every single thing you are going to do, only do it backwards - yes, even that!

Only you have to remember that the day will start at midnight, only instead of going on to one am, you will go back to eleven pm! Just how the hell can you screw backwards?

No, sorry Prof. Hawkin, I think you have got it all wrong this time mate! Unless you know something we don't.

Mind you, maybe we are already doing it backwards, maybe we have already done the whole thing once and we are going back for another shot at it. It just doesn't bear thinking about!

One of the things I want to chuck in here quick in 'money', you know, that thing that it is impossible to have either enough or too much of.

# A CHAPTER ON

## MY OLD GRANDDAD

Now you may not be too familiar with My Old Granddad - unless you are a regular reader of my column in the Felixstowe Town Crier, heaven knows, there is no earthly reason why you should be - but then because of this, and to further enrich your lives, I am going to acquaint you with the old feller!

Gramps - as we used to call him was a typical product of the early nineteen-hundreds. Anything electric, mechanical, or 'dad-blasted newfangled' was seen by him as an invention of the Devil. Not that Gramps was a 'church goin' man', it's just that he had yet to choose sides and he felt nearer to God than the other chap.

We had a sneaky feeling that Gramps had rather a strict upbringing and didn't take too kindly to 'churchin' as he called it.

Gramps wasn't a real old pioneer, but given a few more years back that away he may just have been one. He liked the pioneer days, he thought of the pioneers - his father and grandfather, as real men, men who lived and fought among the Indians, and who scratched a home and a living out of the early bush.

That was the idea, but any thoughts of Gramps 'diggin and scratchin' had died along with the ancestors, "They did all the work, now I'm doing all the restin", he would say, and rest he would.

Gramps has once read a book about Hillbilly folk who sat on their porches in a rocking chair, 'chawed baccy', and spat all over everything; at least he did when Granny wasn't looking, she made him fetch a cloth and wipe it clean!

Granny didn't take too kindly to Gramps 'sittin and rockin' either, and chased him with the broom until he relented and did his chores.

Gramps fancied himself as a bit of a shot with the rifle. True, he could hit the barn, maybe even the cowshed, unless the wind was blowing the wrong way, but when Gramps picked up a rifle, the rest of us cleared out.

Gramps went hunting with some neighbours once. He shot a cow, nearly shot one of the neighbours, and hit a parked car - smashing its windshield, and scared the shit out of the six fellers he was with! They never took him again, but he said he enjoyed himself!

Trouble with Gramps wasn't his aim so much as his eyesight. He claimed there wasn't anything wrong with his eyes, but the truth was he just hated the thought of having to wear glasses, said they made him look 'sissyish'! That is until we took him to see a cowboy film where the hero wore specs, after that we had no trouble with him. Still couldn't shoot though!

Gramps was a pretty good shot, however, with 'baccy spit', give him a wad of baccy and let him chew for five minutes and he could hit a fly at ten feet! Every place on the farm where flies settle was witness to his accuracy - or lack of it!

Gramps earnestly believed that 'too much bathin' will weaken yer', and every now and then Gran would remind him that 'he ain't took a bath for six month or more!' (An exaggeration!) by the simple expedient of chucking a bucket of cold water over him as he sat rocking on the porch. "Damn it all to hell," he would scream, soaking wet and flabbergasted, "what in the name of all that's holy did you do that for?"

"Oops, sorry," she would reply, "must have slipped out of my hand!"

But Gramps got the hint and would scrub hisself clean by dinner time!

Back before we had the farm done up (about twenty years before I came along) there used to be outside privies. These wooden affairs would sit about twenty feet from the house and have to be emptied every now and then. Gramps go so used to using them (there used to be two!) that even after the indoor bathroom and extra downstairs loo was built, he still would go outside and have a pee - not always in the most hidden of venues! In fact, especially after some corn likker and cider, he didn't really give a shit who saw him; he would piddle up against any old tree or fence - another thing that irked Granny no end! And he didn't give a toss who was watching him!

Oh yes, Gramps had more bad habits than you could shake a stick at, but he did have his uses - though Granny never declared any of them to me, still, she did have four kids and she reckoned they were all his!

Gramps was a little bow-legged, not too bad, it just made it difficult to catch pigs, and, believe it or not, catching pigs on a farm was something that happened quite often. If there is a way out of a farm yard or field, pigs will find it. Our job was to find the buggers and bring them back - fifty to a hundred pound porkers can run real fast and wriggle like worms!

Come the village fair one of the games we played was to get into a pen with a greased pig - well greased! and try to catch a hold of it. Think it's easy? Try it!

Gramps, beside not being able to catch pigs, was compensated by an inordinate ability to sit on a horse, had he been alive when the West was Won he would have been either a cowboy or an Indian - depending on the time of day and the amount of free whisky that either one received! However, linked to his inability to shoot straight perhaps his life in the Old West would not have been so glorious after all.

Granny, on the other hand, though scared by loud noises, could shoot remarkably straight for a woman - difficulty being that after taking aim she shut her eyes before firing - about as much use as a fart in a thunderstorm with a moving target!

However, give Gran a scatter gun and she could shoot rabbits till the cows came home!

I remember going on a rabbit drive with Gramps - once! After the first five shots were fired, every time Gramps raised his gun to shoot all other 12 shots dropped to the ground and put their hands over their heads! I found a big tree and stayed there the rest of the drive.

Gramps had a lot of really weird ideas, OK, some of them were probably only weird because that is how I saw them, and, me, being also weird, saw things a lot differently from all other people - well, Gramps any way!

I mean just look at the way he did things. In the farm yard, just south of the cow shed, where we kept the cows in winter and they did their entire milking, farting, shitting etc., we had this enormous pile of cow muck - all mixed up with the bedding straw. One of my jobs, every day, was to muck out these cows, shovel the muck onto a trolley on an overhead track, push the trolley out onto the heap and dump it. Needless to say there was an awful lot of cow piddle in with all this, the cow piddle drained off into a big pit, a big 'uncovered' pit!

Every now and then, in the spring, when we let the cows out and back into the fields, one or two of them would fall into pit and we would have to get a hoist and a tractor and pull them out! Not Gramps, he had another idea, build a wooden ramp, slide it into the pit, and make the buggers climb out! A good idea? Try telling that to the fecking cows! At the end of the first hour of having the ramp in place, four more cows walked DOWN the ramp and joined the one already in the pit! Had I been a little bit bigger and not so scared of Gramps, HE would have gone down the ramp as well!

# A CHAPTER THAT NEEDED WRITING!

Picture the scene. Two thousand plus years ago a bunch of fellas (and some say, a girl) were gathered around a table having a bite to eat. It may have been a curry joint, or even a Chinese, but that is irrelevant now.

One of the people around the table is a bit of a humorist, he is the practical joker in the crowd - every crowd has one, you think about the gang of chums you have and you will recall one!

Anyway, it is just gone seven o'clock and the curry - or whatever- is about to arrive. The weather has been given the once over, as has the political scene,( though in those days one was a little teensy bit careful about how one criticised the government,) all that remained was to get down to the fishing stories ( and one of these fellas had a fishing story to beat them all!) and the odd joke. However, before any of this, one of the guys says, "Just suppose that in about 2,000 year's time, some eejit is looking at this scene, OK, and so let us leave them a little puzzle! For a start, you Jesus, get Mary to hide behind Paul so that no one knows who she is with. Then we will do a few bits of rearranging and see if we can't confuse them. We will write a few puzzles into our stories, each of us telling a different tale; then we will drop a few false clues around, you know, really mix them up! Think of the fun they will have! Some wise guy may even write a book or two about it, or they may even invent something else by then, something that will be like a stage play, with actors, Wow, wish I could live to see it. Another thing, let's give them something to really think about for the next 20 centuries, here, give me that mug you have there Jesus, I will hide this away in a place they will NEVER find it!"

And he did just that!

And so the rest of the curry evening was spent thinking up ways to thoroughly confuse the folk who were to come along in 2, 000 years time. Of course they knew that the future would be full of clever people who could solve puzzles like this. They knew that the clever old chap Leonardo da Vinci would paint a great picture that would be gazed at with awe by people in later years, and they just knew that he, old Leonardo, would be able to know about the secrets they would dream up, and would very cleverly incorporate it all into the painting. I mean he was a fecking genius after all!

But then this whole shebang has got me thinking, what about all the other character in history, how do we know that some bloody great secret isn't set into their painting?

How about "The Death of Nelson" now what could be found in that painting - Nelson's Will? Or a love letter to his sweetheart, or some broad he knocked up while visiting Spain , or France ? The mind boggles!

And how about Michelangelo, all that time he spent on his back in the Sistine Chapel, there must be a wealth of things hidden within those paintings, or is it too much to ask for some nut case to lie on his back studying them!

Then there is the host of paintings Lowry did, the matchstick men and women, and matchstick cats and dogs, come on, look closely, there must be millions of ciphered messages hidden in those paintings, has any one tried fitting all those match sticks into a computer and see that messages are hidden there?

See what I mean, why stop at just one painting, there must be at least another forty films for Tom Hanks to star in. At least another fifty books to be written and fought over.

But I have just one more question about Leonardo's painting, who the picked up the bill for the Last Supper?

Another thing, if JHC wanted to get married to Mary or any other female around at the time, whose business was it anyway?

Hollywood has a lot to answer for. First they make a hero out of all those villains, and boy, were some of them villains! Robin Hood, he really was a hood! Jesse James, Billy the Kid, Dick Turpin, Attila the Hun, Cecil 'have her scrubbed and brought to my tent' Rhodes, George Custer (only good Indian is a dead Indian!) Blackbeard the Pirate, the list is endless, villains every one! Even that old back-stabber Mark Anthony gets his share of glory - Julius, poor sod, really got it in the back!

Even Lassie, I wonder how many postmen (he or she) bit!

Hollywood is really re-writing history. The Yanks win all the wars, it is only a matter of time before the next filming of the Alamo shows the crowd inside winning and poor old Santa Anna gets it chopped off at the gates! Britain should get in there quick and make a film about King George winning the War of Independence and giving

Washington the elbow! That would show 'em, let's show old Georges boat sinking and him drowning as he goes across the Potomac .

Then we could have Admiral John Paul Jones really an English spy working for MFI! I could go on all day, brilliant, let's re-write history a bit more, this is real fun!

# THE GREAT WINTER SPORT CHAPTER

Ice Hockey has always been the only sport I could ever really take seriously, perhaps this next chapter will explain why!

My Grandfather - Gramps, decided that I needed to learn how to ski. In spite of the fact that I showed no interest whatsoever in the sport, Gramps decided that at ten years old I should have another interest other than girls and skating.

I pointed out to him that I had no skis and that all the skis owned by my brothers and sister was too big, and they would never let me use them any how. Not to be outdone Gramps made me a pair of skis.

It took him only a few days in the work shed. The skis were finally produced one Sunday morning when the sun didn't shine and I had already confessed to Gramps that there was too much snow on the pond to skate.

"Come with me, wrap up warm!" he said, so I followed him to the shed. There were the skis.

He had made them out of fairly green maple, machined so that they had a lifted end on the front. He had further bent the heavy, five foot lengths so that they bore an uncanny resemblance to two barrel staves, curved up at both ends. A pair of my older brother's old boots had been glued to the approximate centre of the skis - I say 'approximate' because one boot was about two inches further south than the other one, giving the skis a rather grotesque appearance - and an even more terrifying downhill motion. But there was no doubting the fact that the boots were secure, glued securely heel and toe with the best glue that was available in the 1940's. Just how effective it was would remain to be seen.

We had a ski slope. An area covering three fields and a wood, one we used to tap the maples for sugar and syrup, gave a good downward slope of about 16 degrees with the odd level and the even odder steeper portion!

I had to wear four pairs of socks before the boots felt even the tiniest bit secure, and then the laces had to be wound about my ankles. In real fear and trepidation, Gramps launched me onto the slope. He believed that as I skated and played hockey I should have no trouble balancing. Indeed, if all I had to worry about that day was my balance I would have been laughing!

Gramps, who usually thought of everything, had also made me some ski poles, these were in fact two broom handles, drilled at the bottom and fitted with two pencil sized meat stakes, the handle end had a leather boot lace attached to each one, these, I was informed, this would allow me to steer myself through the trees and through gates that he had thoughtfully opened, and over any bumps in the snow. That was the total sum of my pre-ski lessons. I was taken to the highest point, half a straw stack covered in snow, and launched - without even the benefit of a bottle of champagne!

The first bump I had an estimated speed (well it felt like it to me!) of 30mph, was hiding a cottontail rabbit, which took off almost as terrified as I was. The next bump was not so kind, it was a rock and it hurt!

By the time I came to the first gate I was way off course and somersaulted over the wire, at this point the good Lord must have been watching over me because I landed on my feet, minus one ski pole. I still continued downhill, heading for the other gate, but again, seriously due west of the eastern gate!

By this time I had wet myself and it was cold. My speed had increased to about 45mph and the snow was now too heavy for me to see much ahead of me. I wasn't so lucky with the next fence, but since it was only made of brush I sailed straight through.

The maple wood loomed up through the snow. At this point I found out, the hard way, why skiers used TWO ski poles - and I had only one! You cannot steer with only one, you just go more to one side than the other, the downward motion, the speed, your weight, coupled with gravity, helps correct the direction, and a twenty year old maple completely altered my direction of travel.

Also, at this point, I lost the other ski pole and half one of my skis. The glue held.

I can sometimes recall (usually after a nightmare, at about 2 am) hitting several trees and bouncing off them at speeds that could well be in the 50s or even 60s, but Gramps argues this point saying that I was too young to be travelling on skis at that speed!

I beg to differ, and, sixty years later, I still have the bruises to prove it.

The last obstacle in the way of my downhill plunge was the river, which should, at this time of the year, be covered with no less than 2 or 3 feet of ice. This had been an exceptionally mild winter…

Although I only weighed in at about 80 lbs soaking wet (which I was by now, both with melted snow and pee!) travelling at the great speed that I found myself, and with one and a half, heavy wooden planks glued to my feet, the thin couple of inched of ice proved no match. Fortunately the river at this point was only about two foot deep or I would have drowned. The snow had completely obscured me from Gramps view, the snow also covered any and all the screams and yells I made, and Gramps, even on a bright summers day, would have taken half an hour to reach me had I not been able to drag myself from the fecking cold water!

After that I lived in fear every time I saw Gramps looking at a book or magazine containing pictures of submarines or aircraft.

# THE GREAT HOLIDAY CHAPTER

The first day mother ever drove a car she wound up fifty yards from where she started with the front wheels hanging over the cesspit wall. Another five feet and both Mother and the car would have smelled pretty awful.

Dad never let her drive after that - well she was OK with the tractor, but that was all!

Dad wasn't much better but he sincerely believed he was and that we had to put up with.

Dad's driving was usually to look at someplace, or something, and drive towards it. Anything that got in the way should not have been there in the first place and needed running over or bumping into. In those days, fortunately, there were only about a tenth of the vehicles on the road as there are today, and the cars were made a lot stronger than the rust buckets they churn out now.

Dad, like most men, would never admit that he was lost. He was always taking a 'short cut', or the other favourite, "Who moved that bloody sign?" or, falling that, "This map is a couple of years old at least!"

As a result of all this it usually took us two hours to do a half hour journey.

Canadian roads, even in the nineteen forties and fifties, were pretty good; the signs were adequate, in Northern Ontario and Quebec they were even in French! What more do you want?

That, however, didn't deter Dad, he could get lost even if the roads were signed posted in Latin with English sub-titles!

He loved fishing, did my Old Man, he loved fly fishing and he loved eating the fresh fish he caught, so when we were taken fishing we also had to take a skillet and a box of matches, and the very essential packet of butter in which to fry the freshly caught fish - at least that was the idea. Sometimes the fire would have died out and the ashes turned cold before the first fish appeared, and this was usually too small to eat! Every now and then, though, he - we struck lucky and we could eat trout until our stomachs could take no more. Then we would drive off to find an ice cream parlour and wash it all down with an ice cream soda, and, if we were lucky and he felt in a generous mood, we could have knickerbockers glory or a banana split.

If Dad wasn't in a good mood then we had to make do with a tub of ice cream from the gas station freezer.

Sometimes we would go on boat trip holidays; this involved the hiring of a boat on the river. This also revealed another shortcoming in Fathers training, he was not a good sailor, nor was he a good navigator, which was OK unless the river we sailed on split anywhere and headed off in two different directions, or, as sometimes happened, it split three ways!

Had Dad been with any of the early explorers, we would still be looking for most of the New World and a hell of a lot of the Old One!

My job on board ship was to 'drop the anchor'. The first time I performed this task, on a lake, I dropped the anchor, and, unfortunately, the rope that attached it to the boat. After we had returned to the hire jetty and received a new anchor (having paid - out of my pocket money) for the old one ($75. which was an awful lot of money for someone only getting $20 a month) we returned to the anchorage. After a meal and a bit of fishing, we retrieved the anchor and with it the old one I had just paid $75. for. I got my money back. There is a God after all.

Sometimes our holidays would involve a drive out west, Vancouver, where Mother had a relative, an aunt or something, and this three day trip usually took us a week because of Dad always getting lost (on Highway 2 for Christ's sake!) and Mother's complete inability to read a map. "Why do they always print them upside down?" She would holler.

We drove through some very nice country side and usually past most of the best roadside diners where they sold the best blueberry pie and ice cream. "The one up ahead is much better!" Dad would say. What he really meant was 'by the time we get there you lot will be asleep', or 'it's cheaper!'

We stopped over night at motels, some were good, some were crap, but in those days most cost about five bucks a night for a room, which usually meant someone had to sleep on the couch! Usually me.

Motels had televisions and they always showed Lucille Ball, and a lot of other crap. But at least we were allowed to stay up late so that the next day we would be tired and sleep through most of the rest of the journey so that we didn't see when Dad drove past the best Diners.

Dad wasn't mean; he just didn't like spending money on things that "Mum could make a damn sight better, back home". I was ten before I tasted store-bought bread!

Even older before I tasted 'sliced' store-bought bread!

One of our visits 'South of the Border' involved a long and tiresome drive to the Grand Canyon . As I explained to Dad, had I wanted to sit in the car for three days or more just to look at a big hole in the ground I would have dug a big hole in one of the fields and saved him the time and money, only I didn't swear in front of my Dad or sitting down for the week following said outburst would have been very painful.

OK, so it's a fucking big hole and it took millions of years for the River to wear away all the land that used to fill the big hole, but when you've seen one big hole you've seen them all – (my mind did flick back quickly to Betty Lou Harrison but discretion forbade me to mention her at this time!)

So we fought our way through fifty million other tourists and looked first up and then down at the Grand Canyon. We ate burgers and we drank coke, then we drove all the back to Aunt Joanna's place in Detroit , stayed for a couple of days and drove home. By then I was sick of driving anywhere and just wanted to spend a night cuddled up to cousin Alice (who, had she been around today, would have been labelled a 13 year-old paedophile, but I enjoyed it!)

Holidays are OK if you are about 18 and allowed to drink and spend your own money etc., but being dragged around all over the world when you are only 10 or 12 just isn't fun!

It was many years before I really appreciated holidays, by then it were too damn late!

So there it is the potted history of child who grew up to be a sex-starved, alcoholic day-dreamer.

Apart from spending a few more years searching for hidden codes in ancient books, and wondering why it is when you are dead and have no way of defending yourself everyone wants to write things about you, they did it with Bing Crosby, General Custer, Jesus, Frank Sinatra, my cousin Paddy, and lots of other people, still I suppose it's a lot safer that way, no one can sue you!

Jim Adams

PS: If for some mysterious reason you have glimpsed the first edition of this book - the Proof Copy - you will notice this edition is minus most of the naughty words! I have had to leave a few in to make it read right. My publisher, however, being a God-fearing man (and one who buys me lunch now and then) suggested, quite forcibly, that some folks may prefer the King James Version – so here it is!

Printed in the United Kingdom
by Lightning Source UK Ltd.
118198UK00001B/34-57